EUREKA!

It's Television!

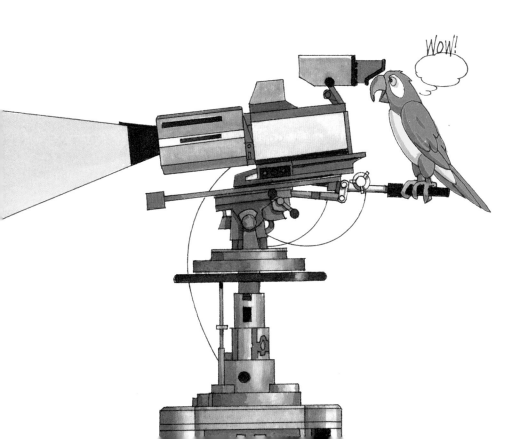

EUREKA!
It's Television!

**BY JEANNE BENDICK
AND ROBERT BENDICK**

illustrations and design by
SAL MURDOCCA

HIGH DESERT MIDDLE SCHOOL
MEDIA CENTER

The Millbrook Press • Brookfield, Connecticut

For Jamie—growing up
in a television world.
J.B.

To my Uncle Joe,
the television man.
S.M.

Note: Words that appear in *italic type* are
defined in the Glossary on page 46.

Published by The Millbrook Press
2 Old New Milford Road
Brookfield, Connecticut 06804

Library of Congress Cataloging-in-Publication Data
Bendick, Jeanne.
Eureka! It's television! / by Jeanne Bendick and Robert Bendick;
illustrations and design by Sal Murdocca.
p.   cm.—(Inventing)
Includes bibliographical references and index.
Summary: Discusses how a television works and the history of
its development.
ISBN 1-56294-214-X (lib. bdg.)
1. Television—Juvenile literature.   [1. Television.
2. Inventions.]   I. Bendick, Robert.   II. Murdocca, Sal, ill.
III. Title.   IV. Series: Bendick, Jeanne. Inventing.
TK6640.B398   1993
621.388—dc20   92-15652   CIP   AC

WHO INVENTED TELEVISION?

How many inventors do you think it took to invent television?

One?
Ten?
A hundred?
A thousand?
Make a guess.
How many years do you think it took to invent television?
Ten years?
Fifty years?
A hundred years? A thousand? More?
Make a guess.

Can you think of some of the things inventors had to find out before they could send pictures and sounds huge distances across space in the blink of an eye?

Almost everything we understand today we know because right from the beginning humans were curious and kept trying to figure things out. In the beginning, everything was a mystery. What made day and night? What were those lights in the night sky? What made the seasons? Where did the sun go? What was lightning?

You know the answers to all those questions so they seem easy. They are not. It took thousands of years of asking, answering, experimenting, and just plain noticing to get those answers.

If you were a really good noticer, sometimes you noticed that you couldn't always believe your eyes.

Back when people still lived in caves, someone surely whirled a torch in a circle and someone else noticed that it looked like a solid ring of fire, instead of a single flame.

This is called *persistence of vision*.

Persistence of vision means that what you are seeing hangs around in your eyes an instant longer than you are seeing it.

A movie is made of separate, still pictures, but they change so fast that you see them as a moving picture. Your eyes are still seeing the first picture when the second one flashes on. Television is also made of rapidly changing still pictures.

If you lived with the cave people, would you have asked yourself how one flame could look like a circle? Maybe not. Most early humans simply accepted the world around them. Others made up myths to try explaining things they didn't understand. A few were really curious. They asked themselves "Why?" and "How?"

Being curious makes a scientist. Are you like that?

Some scientists are inventors, too. Some inventors are also scientists.

Most inventions aren't simple. They depend on something else that had to be invented first.

Wheels had to be invented before anyone could invent a wagon.

An engine had to be invented before anyone could invent an automobile or an airplane.

What do you think might have been the first invention that led to television? Would it be a way to send messages over a distance? What ideas would you have, inventor?

Would you think of drumbeats?

Would you think of smoke signals?

Would you think of reflecting sunlight off something shiny?

Any other ideas?

Some inventors invent things that change the way we live, in small ways or big ways.

A nail was a small invention, but it was certainly important.

Electric lights were a big invention.

So was television.

Before inventors could even *think* about television, they had to discover a lot of other things.

DEAR

MOM

AND

DISCOVERIES ABOUT LIGHT AND SEEING

For a long time most people believed that they could see because their eyes sent out rays, the way a torch lit up a dark place. That was certainly a wrong idea.

In the 11th century, an Arab scientist named Alhazen said that we see because light, reflected from what we are looking at, comes into our eyes. That was a better idea.

In 1666, Isaac Newton, an English scientist, said that light is made of tiny particles emitted, or sent out, from bright objects. He said the particles traveled at great speed. Today we call those bits of light *photons*.

Using a prism, Newton also proved that white light is made up of all colors of light. Do you think that was an important discovery?

Not long after, Christian Huygens, a Dutch scientist, said that light travels in *waves*. (We see different colors because they reflect different *wavelengths* of light.)

ISAAC NEWTON SHOWED WHITE LIGHT, REFRACTED THROUGH A PRISM, IS MADE UP OF RAYS OF DIFFERENT COLORS.

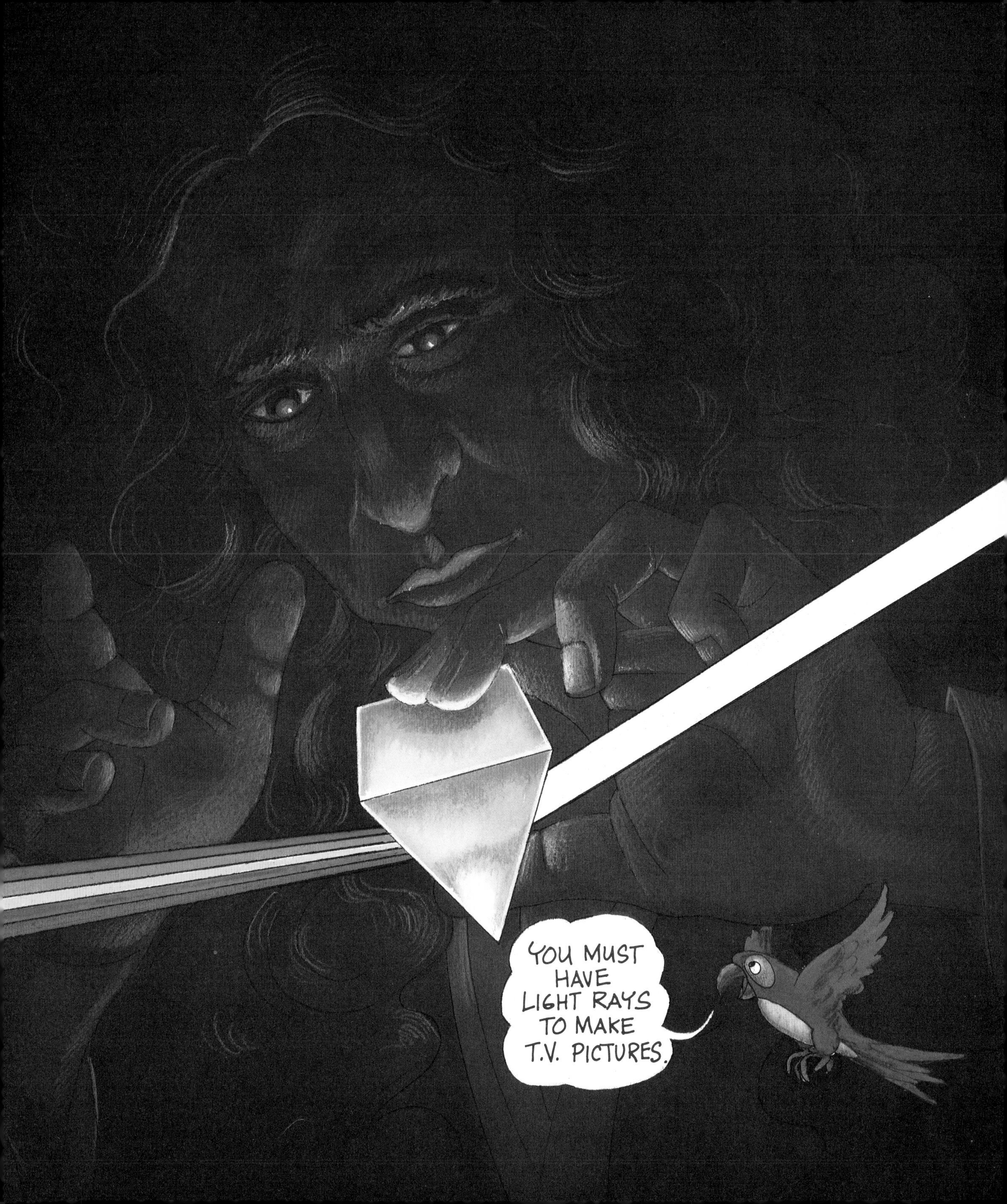
YOU MUST HAVE LIGHT RAYS TO MAKE T.V. PICTURES.

HOW YOU SEE

You see everything in the world because it either makes or reflects light.

Light goes into your eye through the pupil. That's the black spot in the center of the iris, the colored part of your eye. The pupil isn't really a spot. It's the opening into your eye.

The image passes through a lens and is focused on the back wall of your eye. That's called the retina. The retina is made of thousands of tiny nerve cells. They change the light from the scene you are seeing into an image in electricity.

The electric image becomes electric current that travels through your optic nerve to your brain, which changes the electric current back into the scene.

Your brain tells you what you are seeing.

Do you think it ever makes mistakes?

Is seeing always believing? How about the ring of fire?

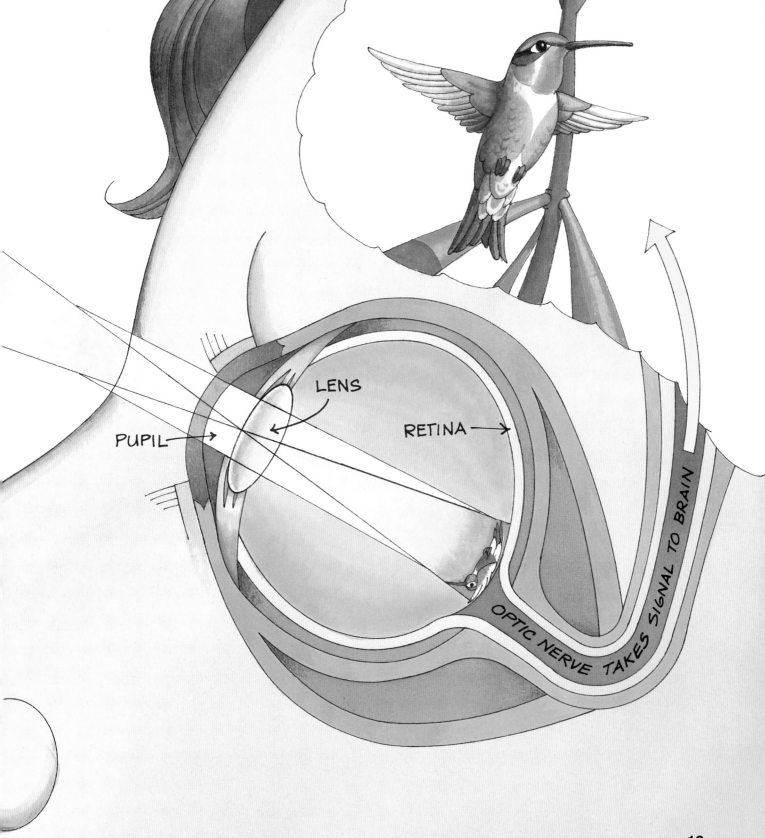

PUPIL

LENS

RETINA →

OPTIC NERVE TAKES SIGNAL TO BRAIN

HOW YOU HEAR

A sound makes the air around it vibrate—jiggle up and down. The vibrations travel through the air in all directions. We call those vibrations *sound waves*. They move through the air to your ears and make your eardrums vibrate. Nerves there change the vibrations into electric currents, which are a copy of what you are hearing. The currents travel through your hearing nerves to your brain, which translates them back into the original sound.

Did you know that you see and hear because of electric currents in you? Do you think that the way you see and hear is anything like the pictures and sounds of television? It is. For television to work, human eyes and ears had to be duplicated.

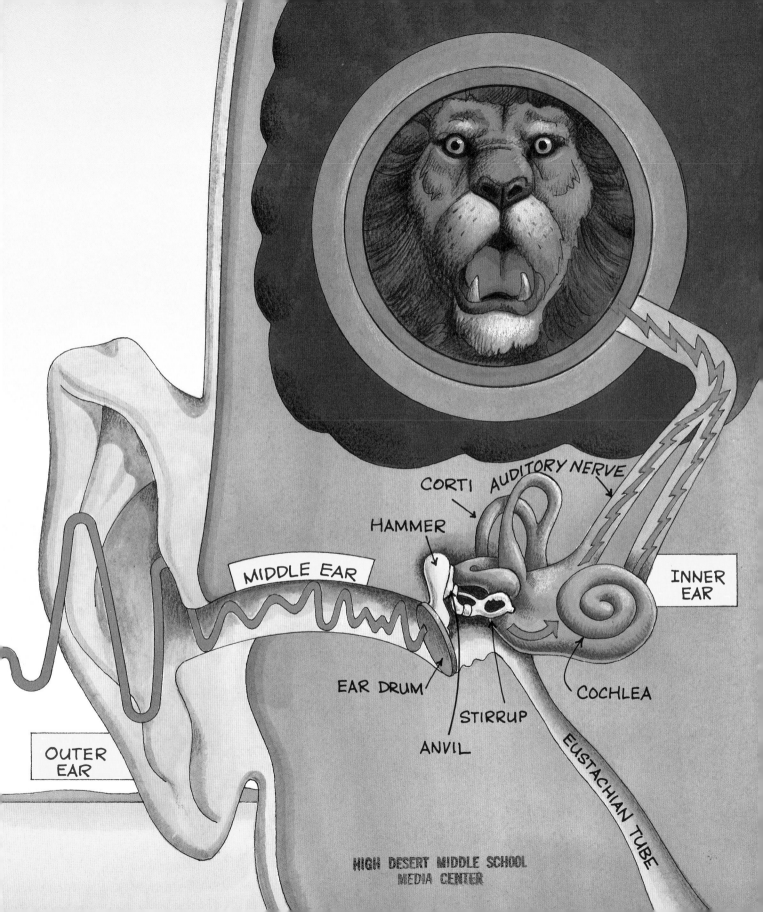

AUDITORY NERVE

CORTI

HAMMER

MIDDLE EAR

INNER EAR

EAR DRUM

STIRRUP

COCHLEA

ANVIL

EUSTACHIAN TUBE

OUTER EAR

HIGH DESERT MIDDLE SCHOOL
MEDIA CENTER

WHAT HAD TO BE DISCOVERED OR INVENTED BEFORE THERE COULD BE TELEVISION

After you know how television works, come back to this part and see if you can figure out why these discoveries and inventions were important.

Three thousand years ago Chinese scientists discovered a kind of very heavy stone that attracted iron. Inventors used those stones to make a compass. A little later, the Greeks discovered magnetic stones, too. Nobody understood what magnetism was.

THEY DIDN'T KNOW HOW IMPORTANT MAGNETS WOULD BE TO T.V.

LIGHTNING IS ALSO STATIC ELECTRICITY.

About 2,600 years ago a Greek scientist named Thales found another kind of "magic" stone. When he rubbed it with his cloak, threads from the cloak and bits of dust and straw stuck to the stone. He thought, because things stuck to the stone, that it was like a magnet. Thales called his stone *Elektron*. (Today we know it as amber.)

With his rubbing, Thales had discovered a kind of electricity called *static electricity*. Static electricity is different from electric current, but it was a discovery. Nobody knew that electricity existed.

In 1600, William Gilbert, doctor to Queen Elizabeth I, made some important discoveries. One was that the Earth is a giant magnet. Another was that magnets have the power to generate, or make, electricity. (We make all the electricity we use today.)

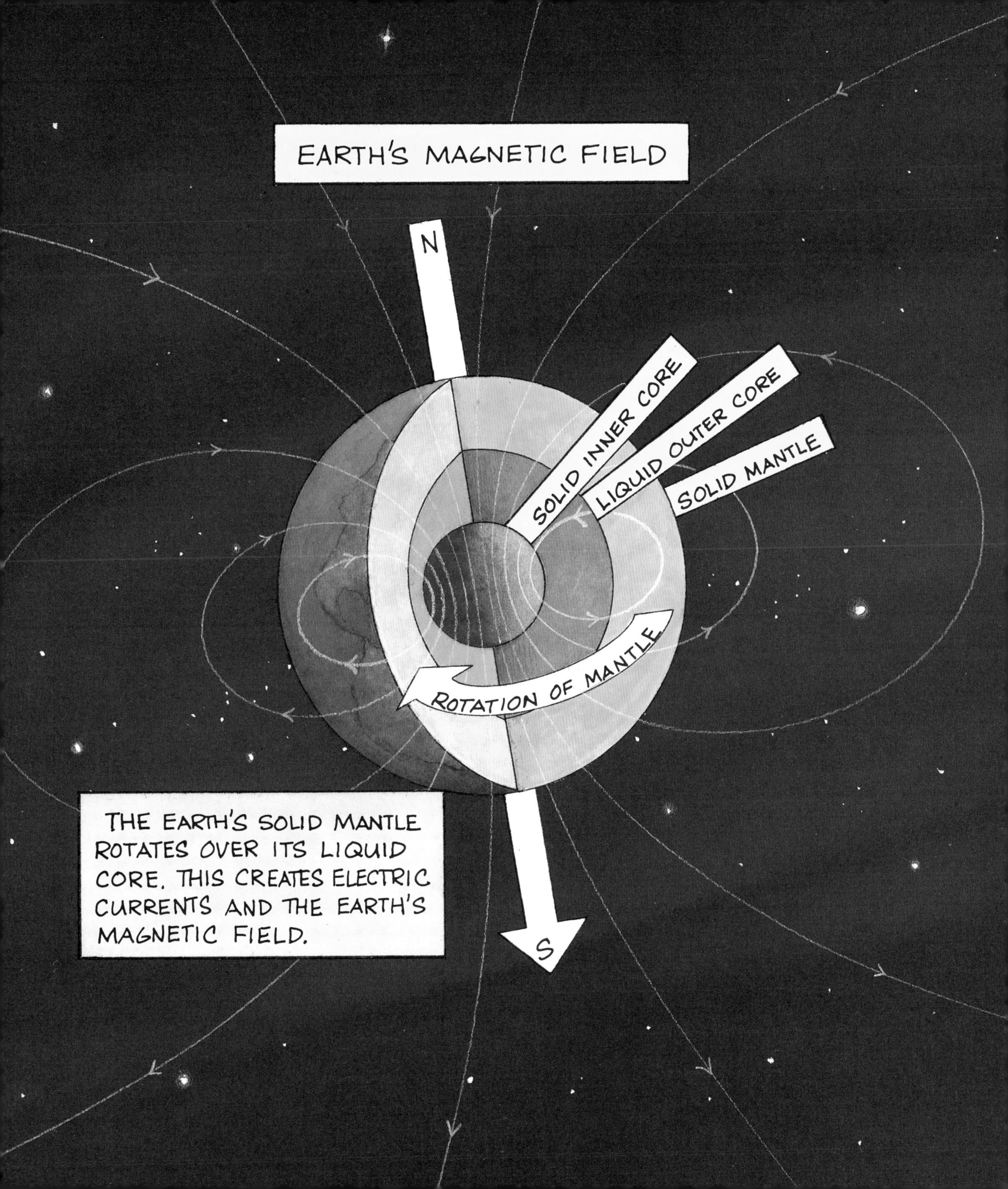

EARTH'S MAGNETIC FIELD

N

SOLID INNER CORE

LIQUID OUTER CORE

SOLID MANTLE

ROTATION OF MANTLE

S

THE EARTH'S SOLID MANTLE ROTATES OVER ITS LIQUID CORE. THIS CREATES ELECTRIC CURRENTS AND THE EARTH'S MAGNETIC FIELD.

Nobody knows who invented the lens, a curved glass that focuses a scene onto a flat surface. (A lens has been found in Assyrian ruins 4,000 years old.)

Italy, 1600: The scientist Galileo used lenses to build a telescope.

Eureka! (*Eureka* is an important word to inventors. It means "I have found it! Hooray! I've done it!")

Through his telescope, Galileo saw the moon clearly. He saw the four largest moons of Jupiter. Most people thought he was tricking them. Who could see anything at such a distance? Nobody could imagine a time when people could watch things happen around the world or in space.

Italy, 1603: Vincenzo Cascariolo discovered *phosphorescence,* a glow of light produced by substances called phosphors when light shines on them.

In 1663, the year before New Amsterdam became New York, Otto von Guericke, a German, built the first machine that could make electricity. It was static electricity, but still, he made it.

At about this time Isaac Newton and Christian Huygens were making their discoveries about light.

In 1745 scientist-inventors discovered how to store a charge of static electricity in a *Leyden jar.* That was an early battery.

LEYDEN JAR

A CONVEX LENS CAUSES IMAGE TO REDUCE IN SIZE.

A CONCAVE LENS CAUSES IMAGE TO INCREASE IN SIZE.

CAN YOU PICTURE A T.V. WITHOUT A LENS?

A few years later, in America, Benjamin Franklin proved that lightning was electricity and that it could be moved from one place to another. He moved a charge from a lightning bolt down a wet kite string and stored it in a Leyden jar. (Don't try that! He could have been electrocuted!)

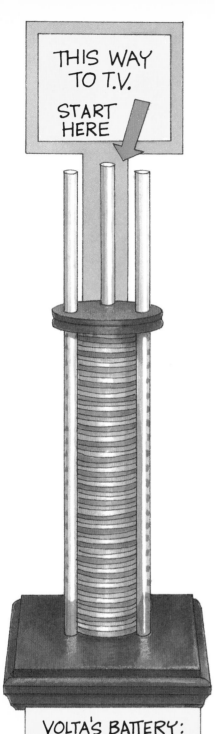

THIS WAY TO T.V.

START HERE

Then, in England, William Watson sent an electric charge through a metal wire 2 miles (3.5 kilometers) long. It seemed to get to the other end the instant it was sent! We know now that electricity moves at the speed of light—186,000 miles (299,337 kilometers) a second.

Italy, 1800: Alessandro Volta invented an electric battery. It changed chemical energy into electric current.

Sweden, 1816: Jons Jakob Berzelius discovered the chemical element selenium. Selenium is *photoelectric*. That means it can change light into electricity. In 1824 he discovered another element, silicon. (Was that important? You'll see.)

England, 1831: Michael Faraday built a dynamo that could make electricity. *Eureka!*

United States, 1837: Samuel Morse invented a working telegraph. It sent messages by electric on-and-off signals.

England, 1837: James Clerk Maxwell discovered that light is a form of energy called an electromagnetic wave.

VOLTA'S BATTERY: STORE ELECTRICITY HERE.

MICHAEL FARADAY: MAKE ELECTRICITY HERE.

MORSE'S TELEGRAPH KEY: BREAK ELECTRICITY INTO SIGNALS HERE.

WHAT WE HAD TO LEARN ABOUT WAVES

What do you know about waves?

Waves in water are only one kind of wave. There are other kinds of waves around us all the time. They are waves of energy. Some are very short and some are very long.

We see some of those energy waves as light.

We feel some as heat.

We hear some as sound.

Radio travels in waves, too. Television pictures and sound are joined with radio waves for their journey across space.

Light and radio waves can travel through the air. They can also travel through empty space. They can travel through a *vacuum*, where there is no air at all.

Sound waves can't travel through a vacuum. They need something to travel through. They can travel through the air, or water, or solids.

Nothing is faster than light waves or radio waves. Sound waves are slower.

THIS WAY, EVERYBODY!

MAKE WAVES HERE

JAMES CLERK MAXWELL

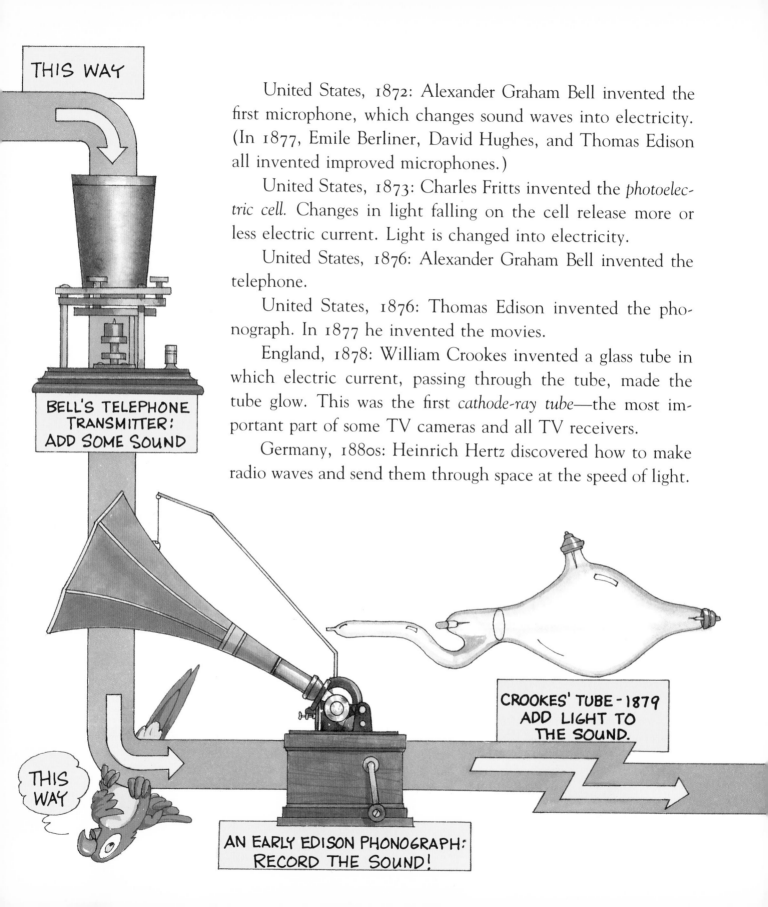

United States, 1872: Alexander Graham Bell invented the first microphone, which changes sound waves into electricity. (In 1877, Emile Berliner, David Hughes, and Thomas Edison all invented improved microphones.)

United States, 1873: Charles Fritts invented the *photoelectric cell*. Changes in light falling on the cell release more or less electric current. Light is changed into electricity.

United States, 1876: Alexander Graham Bell invented the telephone.

United States, 1876: Thomas Edison invented the phonograph. In 1877 he invented the movies.

England, 1878: William Crookes invented a glass tube in which electric current, passing through the tube, made the tube glow. This was the first *cathode-ray tube*—the most important part of some TV cameras and all TV receivers.

Germany, 1880s: Heinrich Hertz discovered how to make radio waves and send them through space at the speed of light.

THIS WAY

BELL'S TELEPHONE TRANSMITTER: ADD SOME SOUND

THIS WAY

AN EARLY EDISON PHONOGRAPH: RECORD THE SOUND!

CROOKES' TUBE - 1879 ADD LIGHT TO THE SOUND.

Germany, 1884: Paul Nipkow invented a mechanical spinning scanning disk. It broke up images into little dots of light that could be changed into electricity.

Italy, 1896: Guglielmo Marconi started inventing radio. In 1901 he sent sound, riding on radio waves, across the Atlantic Ocean. His sending aerial was on a high tower in England. The aerial that received the radio was on a high-flying kite in Canada.

Germany, 1887: K. F. Braun built a much better cathode-ray tube.

England, 1897: J. J. Thomson made a discovery that changed science. He discovered the *electron*, a tiny bit of electrical matter. Electricity is made of electrons. So, for the most part, are clouds, trees, oceans, houses, magnets, cars, and everything else. You are made mostly of electrons, too.

Electrons moving through a wire are electric current. The science of freeing electrons and controlling them to do useful work is called *electronics*.

The 20th century is our century. Ideas and inventions began coming faster. One invention makes the next one possible. Can you see how that happens?

YOU'RE NOT THERE YET!

SIR J.J. THOMSON: ADD ELECTRONS

BRAUN'S TUBE - 1897

MARCONI'S TRANSMITTER: SEND THE SOUND THROUGH THE AIR.

England, 1904: Ambrose Fleming built the first working *electron tube*. The electron tube is a valve. Valves control whatever is running through them. Valves in a water pipe control the flow of water. An electron tube controls the flow of electrons and makes them behave in certain ways.

United States, 1906: Lee de Forest built a better electron tube. He found a way to amplify the current. That means he could take a weak current and make it strong.

Russia, 1907: Boris Rosing designed a way to use the cathode-ray tube to reproduce pictures.

1912, the United States: Edward Howard Armstrong invented a way of recycling radio current for greater amplification. In 1918 he invented an even better system.

1920: Armstrong invented FM. All TV sound is FM.

In 1924, still pictures were sent by radio.

In 1927, AT&T sent pictures and sound from New York City to Washington, D.C., using a mechanical scanning disk. The picture was made of 50 lines.

In 1927, an American, J. A. O'Neill, made the first *magnetic tape* for recording sound. (Tape that could record pictures came about 30 years later.)

FLEMING'S ELECTRON TUBE: HARNESS ELECTRONS HERE.

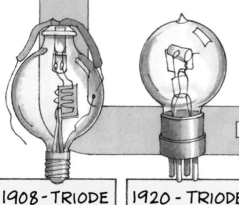

1908 – TRIODE ELECTRON TUBE

1920 – TRIODE PLUG-IN TUBE

BAIRD'S ORIGINAL 1925 TELEVISION CAMERA: A GREAT IDEA, BUT A DEAD END.

In 1928, a Scotsman, John Baird, sent sound and pictures across the ocean, from England to the United States. He called it "seeing by wireless." Baird's system was mechanical.

United States, 1929: Vladimir Zworykin (who had been a student of Rosing's in Russia) patented an electronic television camera tube and television receiver tube.

United States, 1948: Three scientists at the Bell Telephone Laboratories invented *transistors,* the tiny units that direct, control, and amplify the flow of electrons in TV equipment. Transistors replaced all the bulky, hot, fragile vacuum tubes except one—the cathode-ray tube.

Now, all you inventors, let's stand on the shoulders of those earlier inventors and put together a television system. Remember, television is a picture,
then electricity,
then radio waves,
then electricity again,
and finally a picture again
on your television set,
all in an instant.

EUREKA!

TRANSISTOR: TAKE 10 GIANT STEPS!

EARLY CATHODE RAY TUBE

BAIRD'S 1930'S DISC TELEVISION

ON TO ALL ELECTRONIC TELEVISION!

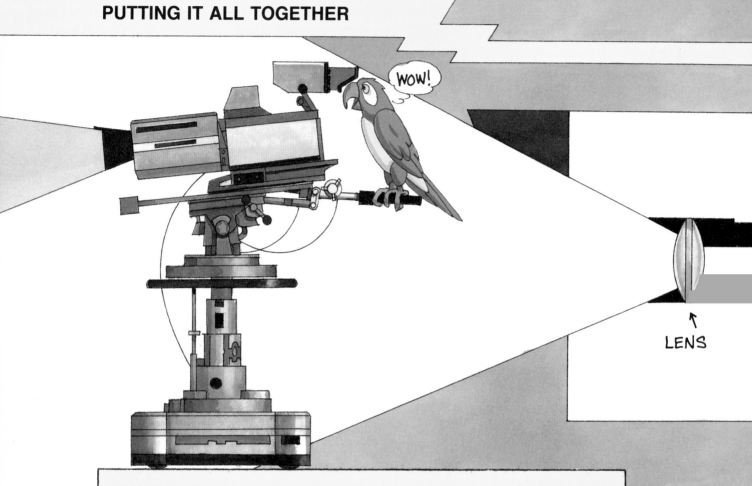

WOW!

LENS

First, the camera. (Hats off to Mr. Crookes, Mr. Rosing, and Mr. Zworykin!)

The TV studio color camera has three cathode-ray tubes in it. A cathode-ray tube is an electron tube in which the electrons flow in a ray, or beam.

As the light image comes in through the camera lens, filters and mirrors split the image into red, green, and blue light. (An apple for Isaac Newton!) Each color of light goes into a different tube.

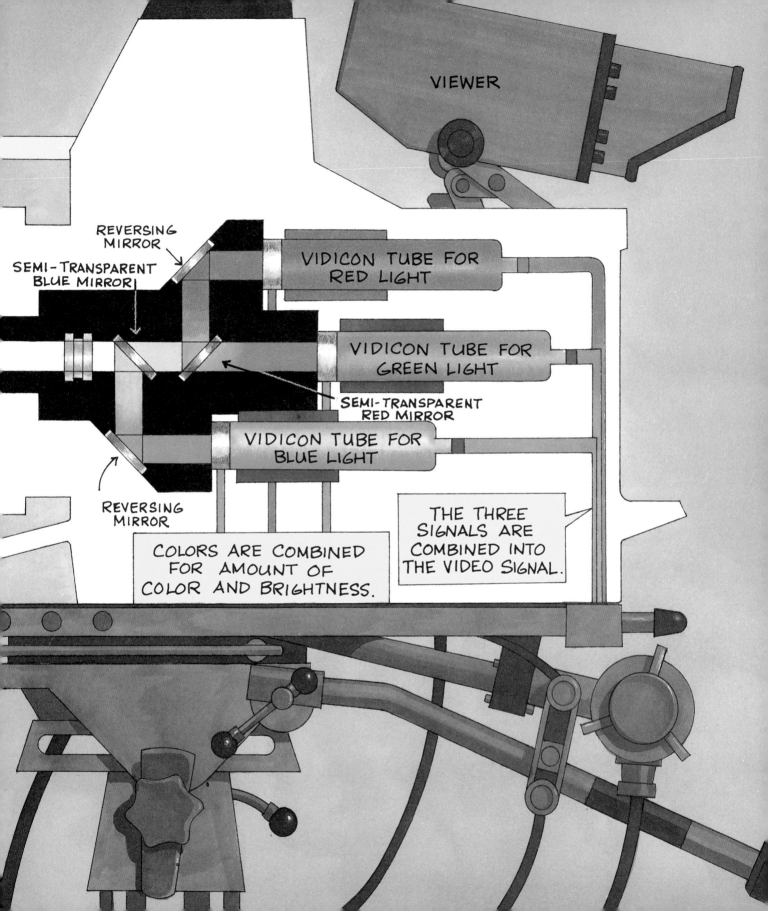

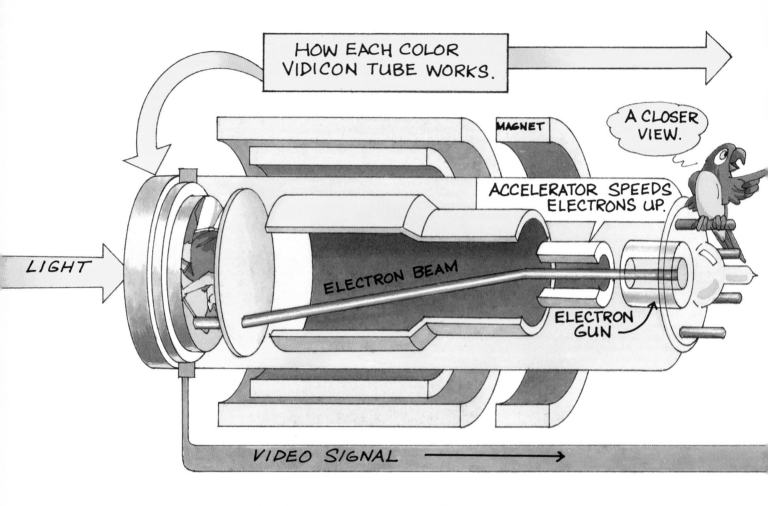

HOW EACH COLOR VIDICON TUBE WORKS.

MAGNET

A CLOSER VIEW.

ACCELERATOR SPEEDS ELECTRONS UP.

LIGHT

ELECTRON BEAM

ELECTRON GUN

VIDEO SIGNAL

As the beam moves across the target screen, each spot grabs back enough electrons to replace the ones it lost. So when the beam bounces back from the target, it varies in strength exactly the way the waves of light did when they came in through the camera lens. Now the beam is an electron picture of that light picture.

The return beam flows out of its tube to join the signals from the other tubes. They are combined and *amplified* (courtesy of Lee de Forest and E. Howard Armstrong). Now they are called the *video signal*. (*Video* means "I see.") Every second, 30 complete pictures in electricity are sent out of the camera.

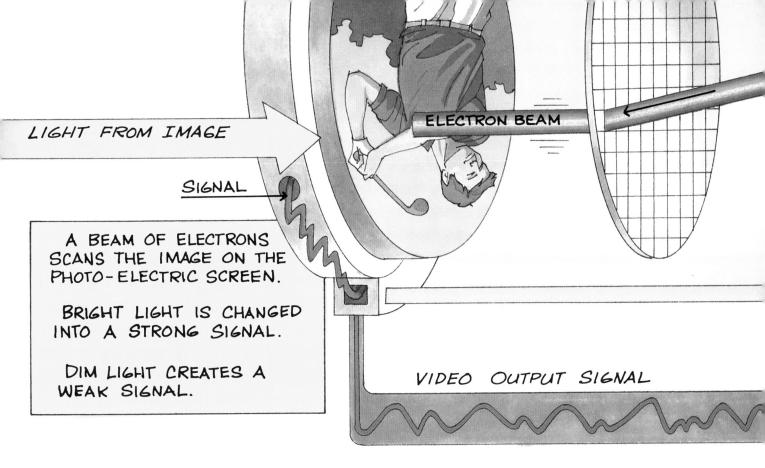

LIGHT FROM IMAGE

SIGNAL

ELECTRON BEAM

A BEAM OF ELECTRONS SCANS THE IMAGE ON THE PHOTO-ELECTRIC SCREEN.

BRIGHT LIGHT IS CHANGED INTO A STRONG SIGNAL.

DIM LIGHT CREATES A WEAK SIGNAL.

VIDEO OUTPUT SIGNAL

The sound, which is called the *audio signal,* is added. (*Audio* means "I hear.")

At one end of each tube there is a screen made of thousands of tiny, photoelectric spots. (Three cheers for Charles Fritts!) As light falls on each spot, it gives off electrons. (Hooray for J. J. Thomson!) The brighter the light is on that spot, the more electrons jump out.

At the other end of the tube is an *electron gun,* controlled by *electromagnets.* (If only Sir William Gilbert could see it!) The gun shoots a beam of electrons at the target screen. The beam *scans* the screen, moving across it the way you read a book, but much, much faster. It scans the entire screen of 525 lines 30 times a second.

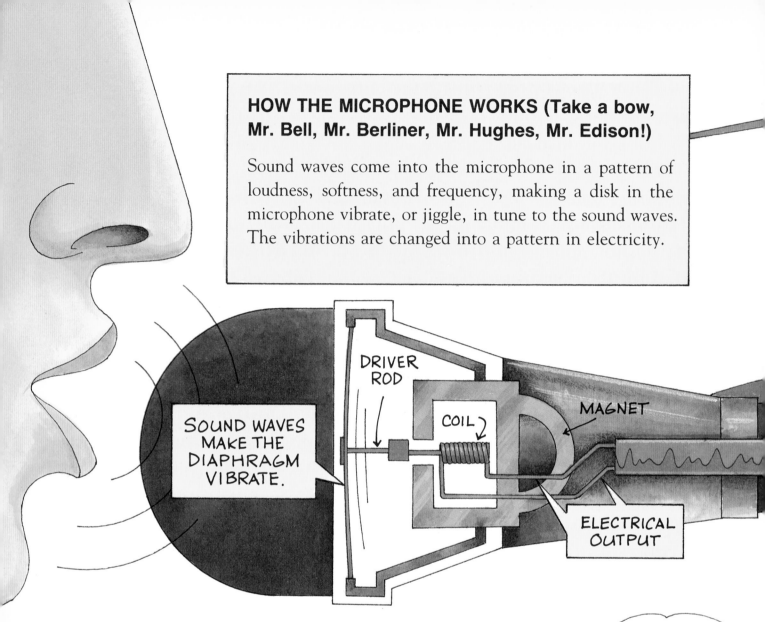

HOW THE MICROPHONE WORKS (Take a bow, Mr. Bell, Mr. Berliner, Mr. Hughes, Mr. Edison!)

Sound waves come into the microphone in a pattern of loudness, softness, and frequency, making a disk in the microphone vibrate, or jiggle, in tune to the sound waves. The vibrations are changed into a pattern in electricity.

DRIVER ROD

COIL

MAGNET

SOUND WAVES MAKE THE DIAPHRAGM VIBRATE.

ELECTRICAL OUTPUT

SOUND MAKES DIAPHRAGM VIBRATE. DIAPHRAGM IS CONNECTED TO COIL, LOCATED BETWEEN POLES OF A MAGNET. THIS GENERATES TINY AMOUNTS OF ELECTRICITY THAT MATCH THE PATTERN OF THE SOUND WAVES THAT MOVED THE DIAPHRAGM.

NOW YOU CAN HEAR ME.

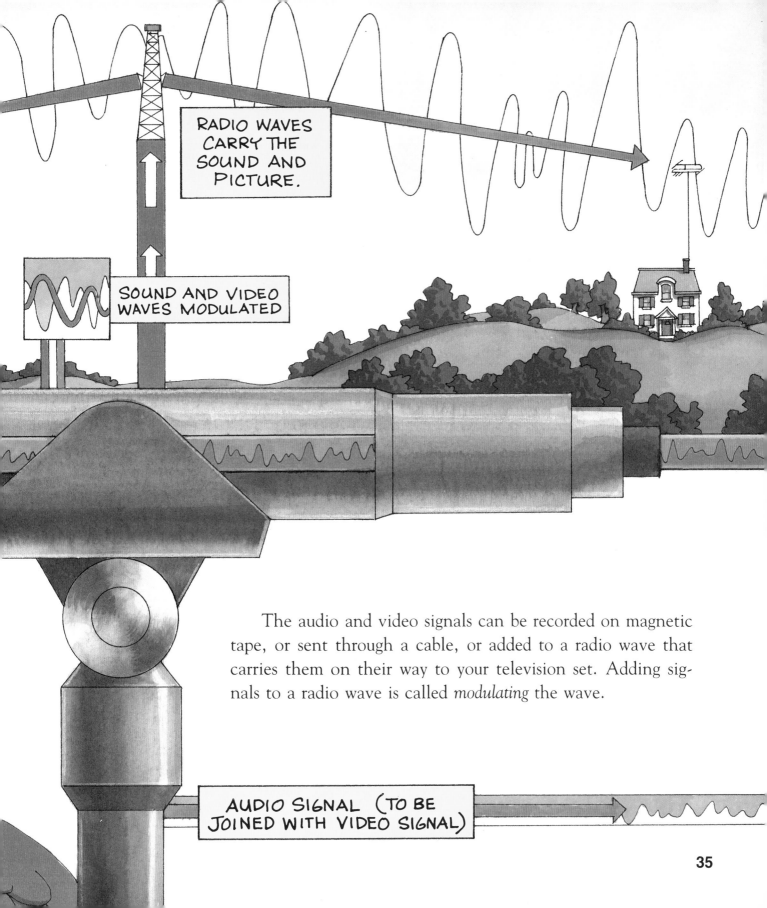

RADIO WAVES CARRY THE SOUND AND PICTURE.

SOUND AND VIDEO WAVES MODULATED

The audio and video signals can be recorded on magnetic tape, or sent through a cable, or added to a radio wave that carries them on their way to your television set. Adding signals to a radio wave is called *modulating* the wave.

AUDIO SIGNAL (TO BE JOINED WITH VIDEO SIGNAL)

ANOTHER KIND OF CAMERA
(Hooray for Jons Jakob Berzelius!)

Most TV news and sports stories are shot on location, where the action is. Also, many people like to have their own home TV cameras. So inventors came up with small, rugged, hand-held cameras that get their electricity from batteries. (Thank you, Alessandro Volta.) These cameras do not have cathode-ray tubes.

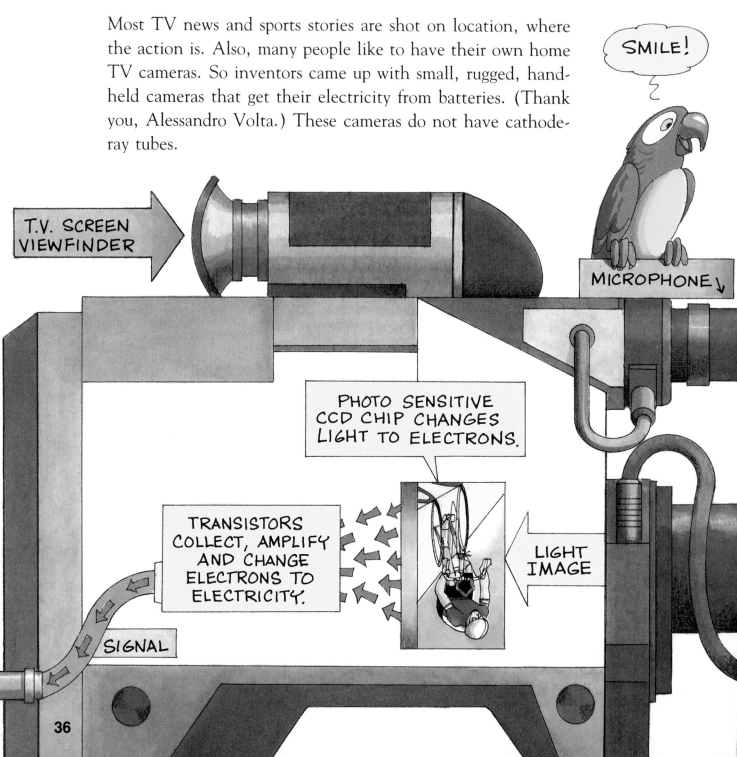

SMILE!

T.V. SCREEN VIEWFINDER

MICROPHONE ↓

PHOTO SENSITIVE CCD CHIP CHANGES LIGHT TO ELECTRONS.

TRANSISTORS COLLECT, AMPLIFY AND CHANGE ELECTRONS TO ELECTRICITY.

LIGHT IMAGE

SIGNAL

Light from the scene comes in through the camera lens and falls on a screen made of thousands of tiny silicon, photoelectric cells that are arranged in evenly spaced rows. (This screen is called a CCD, which stands for charge-coupled device.)

The cells change the light into electrons, which are scanned off by sensors in the same order and strength as the light waves from the scene. Every second, 30 images in light are changed into 30 images in electricity as they flow out of the camera.

At the same time a microphone, either hand-held or in the camera, records the sound on magnetic tape. (You did it, Mr. O'Neill.)

Whether the picture, with its sound, comes from a studio camera or a battery camera, now it's ready to be added to a radio wave, or sent through a cable, or recorded on magnetic tape.

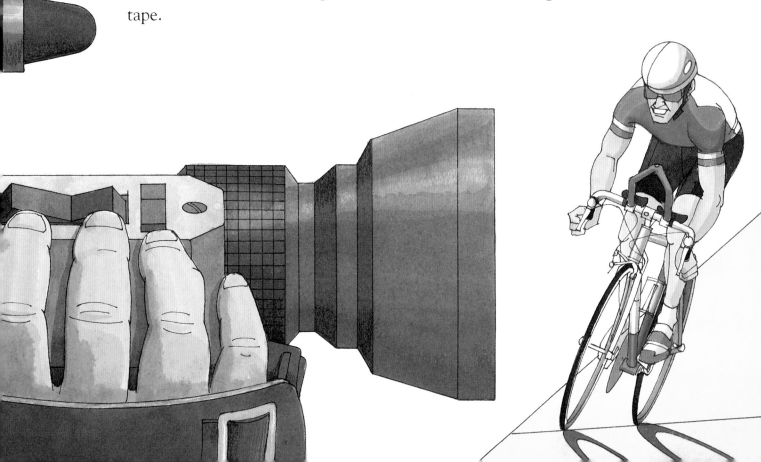

WOW!

CABLE COMPANY DISTRIBUTES PROGRAMS FROM ALL OVER.

CABLE TELEVISION →

HOW THE SIGNAL IS SENT

Broadcast Over the Air

Before the signal that is the sound and the picture can be sent over the air, it has to be joined with the radio waves that carry it. (We salute you, Mr. Hertz and Mr. Marconi!)

Local TV stations broadcast the signal from a high antenna, because the kind of radio waves that carry TV travel in straight lines. They can't go farther than 60 or 70 miles (96 or 112 kilometers), because they do not curve around the Earth.

Your antenna at home grabs the signal out of the air. Which signal it grabs depends on which channel your set is tuned to. Your television set separates the signal from the radio wave and feeds it to the television picture tube and the speaker in the set.

WOW!

WOW!

WOW!

Through a Cable

If you get your TV through a cable, the electric signal never has to be changed into radio waves. It flows through the cable to your set.

By Satellite

Many TV signals are carried over very long distances by radio waves. First they are *up-linked* to TV relay satellites. These satellites are in position 22,300 miles (35,880 kilometers) above the Earth. (Higher and higher, Mr. Marconi!) Because they orbit the Earth at the same speed that Earth is orbiting, they are always in the same places over the Earth. The satellites receive the signals, amplify them, and send them back to Earth on a radio wave of a different frequency so they don't interfere with incoming waves. On Earth they are picked up by receiving dishes in many places. (Sending the signals back to Earth is called *down-linking*.)

The signal from a satellite can be rebroadcast from a TV station antenna, or sent through a cable, or picked up directly by a receiving dish on a house or in a yard.

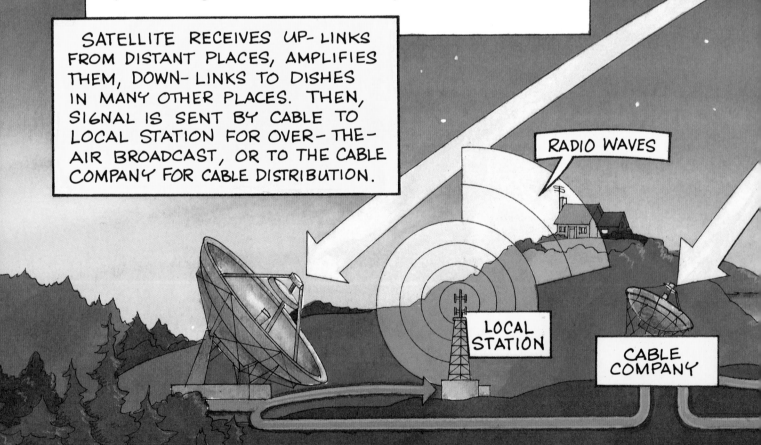

SATELLITE RECEIVES UP-LINKS FROM DISTANT PLACES, AMPLIFIES THEM, DOWN-LINKS TO DISHES IN MANY OTHER PLACES. THEN, SIGNAL IS SENT BY CABLE TO LOCAL STATION FOR OVER-THE-AIR BROADCAST, OR TO THE CABLE COMPANY FOR CABLE DISTRIBUTION.

RADIO WAVES

LOCAL STATION

CABLE COMPANY

WATCH THIS!

HOW YOUR TV SET WORKS

It's no good to invent a television camera unless you invent a television receiver. You can't shout "Eureka! Television!" unless you have both.

The receiver lets you choose the TV signal you want out of the many signals your antenna can pick up. You do that by switching to the channel you want to watch.

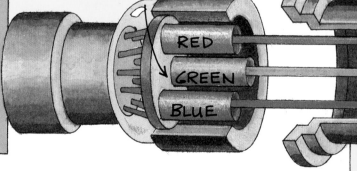

THREE ELECTRON GUNS

LUMINANCE DETECTOR CONTROLS COLOR BRIGHTNESS.

CHROMINANCE DETECTOR AND TRANSISTORS CONTROL THE THREE COLORS IN EACH PART OF THE PICTURE.

RED
GREEN
BLUE

SYNCHRONIZATION DETECTOR MAKES TUBES SCAN TOGETHER

SYNCHRONIZATION SIGNAL

SOUND DETECTOR

The cathode-ray picture tube is the most important part of the TV set.

At one end of the tube are three electron guns, a red one, a green one, and a blue one. These shoot their electron beams to the other end of the tube, scanning a metal plate with thousands of holes in it.

The three color beams go through each hole and fall onto a screen that is coated with thousands of tiny strips of red, blue, and green phosphors. (A bright idea, Mr. Cascariolo!)

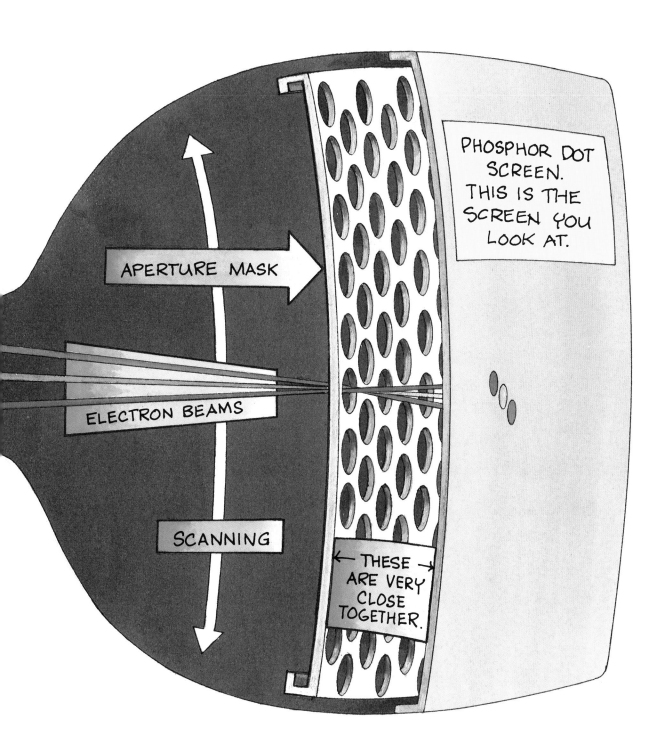

The electrons from each color gun make the phosphors of their own color glow with the same brightness as the picture that came into the camera. The guns scan the screen in the same order as the guns in the camera scanned the screens there. (If you look carefully, you can see the lines that make up the picture. You don't have to count them.) Thirty pictures a second appear on your television screen, but your eyes aren't fast enough to see each one. Persistence of vision! (You saw it first, cave people!)

Now we have a picture window on the world.

Eureka! Television!

Great work, all you inventors!

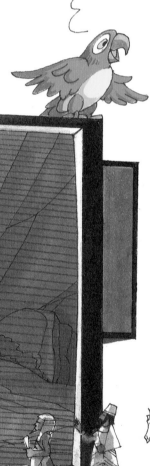

I GUESS EVERYBODY HELPED.

OPTICAL GLASS FIBER CABLE

INVENTORS ARE WORKING ON THESE THINGS

A way of breaking down the TV signal into smaller and faster bits so it can be transmitted faster with more detail and more special effects. These on-and-off signals are a *digital system*. (Does that sound like Samuel Morse's telegraph?)

A way of making the picture sharper by scanning more lines for each picture. This is called *high-definition* TV, and it would have twice as many lines as we have now—525 lines in the United States. (How sharp do you think that first 50-line picture was?)

A way of using light to send TV signals through a cable made of glass or plastic threads. Photons are much easier to control than electric current in a wire cable. This is called *fiber-optic transmission*. (Do you think Isaac Newton could ever imagine sending his light particles through a cable?)

Bigger, flatter TV receiver screens that can be hung on a wall. Do you think receivers can be made without bulky tubes? Could transistors take their place?

Interactive television. Would you like to communicate with the programs you are watching? How would you use that kind of TV?

They're working on person-to-person television,
3-D television,
wristwatch television.
What would *you* invent?

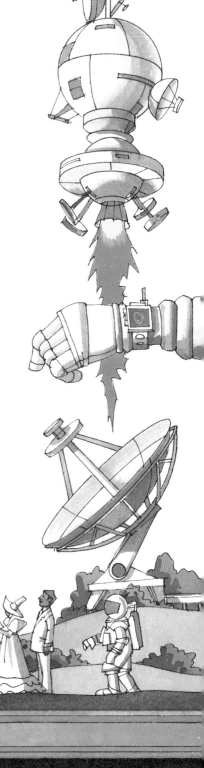

←—LIGHT SIGNALS IN INNER CORE

GLOSSARY

Amplified. Strengthened.

Audio signal. An electric signal mixed with the sound signal.

Cathode-ray tube. An electron tube in which electrons flow in a beam that makes a screen in the tube glow.

Digital system. A way of breaking TV signals into smaller and smaller bits.

Down-linking. Sending signals from a satellite back to Earth.

Electromagnet. A device that is magnetized by electric current surrounding it.

Electromagnetic wave. A wave of energy. Light waves and radio waves are electromagnetic waves.

Electron. A tiny bit of electrical matter. Everything is made of electrons. Electrons flowing together are electric current.

Electron gun. Part of a cathode-ray tube that shoots a beam of electrons at a target.

Electron tube. A vacuum tube in which electrons are controlled.

Electronics. The science of harnessing electrons and putting them to work.

Fiber-optic transmission. Sending the signal in the form of light waves through cables made of glass or plastic threads.

High-definition TV. Making TV pictures much sharper by doubling the number of lines that make up the picture.

Leyden jar. A device for storing an electric charge.

Magnetic tape. Plastic ribbon coated with a magnetic substance that lets it pick up and record sound or picture signals.

Modulating. Adding a signal that changes the pattern of electric current, light waves, or radio waves.

Persistence of vision. What you are seeing stays in your eyes for an instant longer than you are seeing it.

Phosphorescence. A glow of light produced by substances called phosphors when light shines on them.

Photoelectric. Being able to change light into electricity.

Photoelectric cell. A device that changes light into electricity.

Photons. Tiny particles of light.

Radio wave. A form of electromagnetic wave.

Scanning. The movement of an electron beam across the screen of a cathode-ray tube.

Sound wave. A vibration in the air caused by a sound.

Static electricity. An electric charge that cannot be changed into electric current.

Transistor. A tiny device that can direct, control, and amplify the flow of electrons.

Up-linking. Sending a signal from the ground up to a communications satellite.

Vacuum. A place where there is no air.

Video signal. Light waves that represent the picture, mixed with electric waves.

Wavelength of light. The distance from the peak of one light wave to the peak of the next one. We see different colors because they reflect different wavelengths of light.

Waves. Energy in motion.

INDEX